In Search Of Light

Varghese J Kuttikat

Dedicated to my children

Anoop & Carine

Ambili & Nithin

Wake Up Into Morning

May   the   entire   Universe   wake up into Morning

Each of   us daring enough   to proceed, braving

Fire and brimstone, in togetherness   benign

All our inventiveness   focused on   common   boon

Mounting   mighty defence   militant   against   foul   whispers   sullen

Unloading   all possible   individual   sweetness and light new-born

Yes, let every one of us sing alone   as well as in legion

Let us be   warriors of Light, driving away   doom   and din

Let   us   delightedly   sing   of   peace, love and hope   heaven- born

We have   reason   to celebrate; here   are sure signs of deliverance

Grateful

I do salute my ancestors and the powers benign

That set me firm and serene on a designed plane

When tempests raged all around and beasts danced damned

I find reason; valid signs to believe in hope militant

Because those who join me on the line are mightily blest

I do believe the present maligned state would vanish indeed

The World would bloom forth in glory real radiant

And Man would greet the World with light in his eyes

Milk and honey would be everybody's very own

Hate and beastliness would be buried for ever and ever

The miracle happens; Man finds himself in the company of brethren

Deliverance, O Deliverance, At Last

A vile virus tiny

Yet monstrous enough

To smother the entire breath human

Burns with lust

To corrupt the human flesh

With hideous, murderous design

This dark beastly romance

Has already made a conquest

Agonizingly inhuman

Its cruel dazzle and aura seductive

Has not yet met with

Any holistic human defence

Convincingly holy and impeccably hygienic

To undo the spell real lethal

O awake, arise, saviours, saints spirited

All duly acclaimed or yet to be acclaimed

Human heroes for their healing touch benign

Blessed angels rich, human to the core, pouring in

Soothing balms, superfine oils and aromatic scents enliveningly serene

Are you up above or down below or right round the corner?

All at once, yes, right now, rush in the launch mighty redemptive

What holds you back?

Is it that you are not still in possession of the potent dispeller,

The dispeller mighty of the specific foulness, maliciously infectious

Welcome to you all, of all shades, of all hues, of all syllables, of all statures

Let all of us be comrades in an all-out heroic human attempt

To keep breathing with ease and elan, with lifted up hearts and heads,

Smashing out the tiny virus, treacherous, for ever and ever

This is a throbbing drive, a major, essential purge urgent

Exalted be the purge and its entire accent on deliverance human

O, the triumphant, exultant notes in praise of deliverance

And the emergent glow radiant projects morning hope-lit

Long awaited, longed for, worthy to be saluted, convincing man at once of his might and tininess

Brethren, seniors, young ones, little ones, each and everyone

Come out of your segregated cells of suffocation where you lived dead

Cheer up, breathe in and breathe out confident and move about free in the world

The bloody infection had mutilated the living world into isolated hells of horror

Glorious signs of the humanity purged and guarded against collapse inspire hosannas

Fire tongued

Fire tongued utterances of the Lord,

O Bounty bounteous, blossom out

In cadences compellingly candid

That the entire human lot readily respond

With harp and lyre, singing and dancing around

The arduous note of command thunders forth

Nevertheless, the illuminated mind seizes the benignness implied

Awesome syllables rush out from the devotees' lips

Gradually picking up eloquence intense

Yet some just whisperings, yet others thunderous

O Lord, may my whisperings be temptingly beauteous

Utterances lordly, full of majesty, resounding all varied notes

Wonder Reverent

O LORD, give me an inexhaustible theme,

 A theme I can celebrate,

A theme Sunny and resplendent

Something to thunderously wonder about

And keep me in a state of perpetual wonder reverent

A sudden avalanche of sparks awakens me,

The illumination blest prompts me to beseech:

"O Lord, don't dazzle me,

Order this light in cadences soft"

I crave vision magnificent and eloquence extravagant

The serenity to extol both eloquence and silence

And finally to accept the constitution of silence,

If it is inevitable, and yet preserve the blooming, ceremonial voice

Angels & Demons

Could angels and demons share the same breeze?

Won't it disturb the Universe entire

If gods and demons dance together?

Not conciliation, but combat is the way to soar,

Yes, the way to soar up, to soar up the heavens

Yet the desire to retire sometimes surges up in humans

Spirited eloquence gradually, consistently slides into silence

Saints seize the heavens awesome, as they are ever ready to descend downwards

Edenic Grace

O All-Seeing Eye, illuminate my mind

To drink in the nectar of things exceedingly beautiful

And ecstatically extol the Master Designer masterful

All the while aspiring to beam in or designer resourceful

Just as a devotee in rare moments gets elevated to be a god graceful

This transfiguration is the miracle the devotee experiences awful

The sky of the Self gets sunny and resplendent, real ethereal

All thoughts of doom flee away, the vales get exalted eminently

Transcendent vision of star-dazzle soars up majestically

As oft, balmy breeze fondles me, inducing in me Edenic grace blissful

Wakefulness

I sing spiritedly in ecstasy of love

I soar up as I sing and as I salute the heavens above,

The sheer brilliance of the skies sets me on the waves of awe

Sometimes dazzles me, shooting an agony of trance

Into the core of my being, wonder thunderous

Seizes the Self, setting aside all earlier premonitions

Earlier, I had been crucified and buried, may be I experience surges,

Yes, surges of resurrection tremendous, the entire Universe

Holding me aloft, I no longer crave easeful sleepiness

But welcome wakefulness beneficent, where my brethren join me in salutation

Get Beyond Time

May sobering thoughts elegantly rush in

Driving away cloudy, stormy, unsettling ones

It pleases Time to display its versions various

It can be seemingly evanescent, as it can be ever existent

Both creator and destroyer, it can be rejuvenating as well as paralyzing

Angel and demon, soothing and terrifying, benevolent and malevolent

Significantly tremendous, at once fleeting and lasting, important

Mighty, graceful benefactor, formidable, heartless villain

Relentlessly unappeasable, fastidious, indifferent

Overridingly capricious, respecter of none

Sometimes uttering "hosannas", sometimes venomous, murderous cries

Nonetheless, inescapable, weaves webs manifold, not easy to deal with

Get beyond Time if you can, you experience eternity in a moment

The Human Eloquence

Lifting up   voice   for causes   solemn

Can't be   condemned   sound   and fury mean

In fact, its eloquence, eminently human

To be equated   with thunder divine

The ever   gentle Jesus   thundered out;

"Don't make my Father's house a market place damned"

Felicity   of Eden or bliss   heavenly attainable failed

To forestall the   tragic fall of Man into the sorriest pit

Hence   the commandments with the accent on consequences   bloodiest

Exalt Existence

When I bid adieu to this scene sunny, glorious,

Equally glorious or even more glorious scenes would greet me

When I express this wish, I visualize derisive smiles shot at me

With public denunciation, declaring me a victim of vanity,

A vain idle dreamer, an absolute Zero, definitely on the decline

I boldly dream of mortality slipping into immortality, a fond dream human

None can forbid me my wild longings hallowed which the entire Humanity yearn

Of all beings, Man is perhaps the only being privileged to dream magnificent, solemn

Man can sing and soar up, either singly or in chorus, hilariously serene

Exalt existence with harp and lyre, lit with awe, love genuine

Fallen Angels

In a way, we are all fallen angels, fallen from grace

O LORD, you created us humans in your image, says the Scriptures

Did you conceive, us O Lord, a little less than angels,

Or far greater, more glorious than the winged ones?

In fact, what provoked their burning bitterness?

In some blessed moments, O Lord, we sing our songs glorious

Sometimes full of inspired, hilarious, winged songs

Sometimes, we sing in an agony of trance, recognizing our uniqueness

In our vanity, we sing and soar up, let us persist in our sweetness

We shall be reduced to dust, yet we dream the dust would bloom in bliss

Miracle Of Life

Holy stirs dance about flooding the Self

I salute the Absolute awesome

Salutations to Thee, O Light incorruptible

I beseech Thee, O Lord, not to dazzle me

But to pour out Thy brilliance in cadences benevolent

That my senses open out sufficient to stand rapt in delight

Drinking in the beauty of the all mysterious Universe

And the nobler, austere beauty of human existence

Despite the stormy dark avalanches of angst

Is it an eloquent murmur or thunderous illumination:

I have been awakened into a mighty revelation:

Life is a miracle, be worthy of the miracle of life

Desires Forgivable

Sudden vanishings stir up vibrations intense

Very much alive, those who remain salute the departed ones

Brevity of earthly sojourn needn't dishearten us

All blossoming lapses into withering dolorous

The eloquent flutist surrenders his flute and himself

With a sense of fulfilment, saluting the Absolute awesome

Let me soar up into wakefulness beyond sleep

Forgive me, if my wish be extravagant, full of pomp

Nevertheless, O Lord, Thou art Bounty bounteous

And would grant us our hearts' forgivable desires

The Healing Touch

Though the flesh is weak, the spirit is ready and willing

Solitary songs as well as songs in chorus dwell in me ringing

May be vanity, I am confident there is something beyond sound and fury

My notes are simply waves on the surging ocean, yet they are surging

I am grateful to Bounty infinite that I am alive and singing

Perhaps my lyrical notes lack beauty or charm, still I sing

Though brief, my brethren and I be allowed intense singing

Thou granted sweetness to my anguished syllables raging

Thy all- healing touch lent my entire singing great effect soothing

Notes Ecstatic, Notes Grievous

I do get ecstatic, as I listen to birds

Outpouring their selves, unloading sometimes

Surges of sheer delight, sometimes unrelieved sorrows

Ecstatic notes as well as notes grievous stir up my deeps

And I wonder if grievous notes excel the cheerful ones

In pure aesthetic beauty appealing to our intimate chords

Only perverse beings would embrace distress with fondness

We aspire to the heights of heavenly bliss

And sing spiritedly of holy mountains majestic with perfect ease

It is human glory uniquest that we can also sing of our bleakest valleys

The Conquest

If everything throws you into ecstasy extreme,

Thrice blessed are you, really elect, indeed rare

If you can revel in your being, despite brimstone and fire

You are the crowned martyr whom angels extol with harp and lyre

If pain and peril can't daunt you, , you can sing and soar

Even when the skies are dense, cloudy and swelling sore

And as you soar up, the skies would turn markedly azure

Angels benevolent would salute you and declare you a pioneer

Guard Against Blasphemy

Heaven as an abounding abode of bliss:

Isn't it sufficient inducement to virtue bounteous?

To excel a larkin singing ecstatic notes:

Won't it prompt humans towards perfect blessedness?

Why one should be frightened with fire and brimstone

Lest one should fall into pits perilous, victim of temptation?

Why do Thou permit O Lord, bitter weeping?

And gnashing of teeth, again and again recurring?

O Bounty infinite, guard us against blasphemous inclinations

Wondering if Thou art in conspiracy against the anguished souls

Longing Of The Human Lot

May my wild imaginings, rosy and resplendent

Lift me up and let me exult, hope-lit

When I awaken the dawn with harp and lyre, love-lit

The entire Universe exults and I revel in the core of being exalted

Voices benign thunder forth: "rejoice and celebrate the light

Subtle whisperings insinuates: "you are a victim of vanity unlimited

You may soon be thrown into bottomless pit, totally unlit "

O Lord omnipotent, banish gloominess altogether and let me exult

Set my heart aright and keep it throbbing in cadences of light

My vanity be blest, it is a power-packed longing of the entire human lot

Sleep Or Wakefulness

However intoxicating the dream, real beautiful

Don't let me lapse into sleep eternal

It is dreams, though, maybe, a bit unbeautiful

And sometimes mingled with bitter sobs doleful

That I would love to indulge in, fully awake, mindful

Though night might be lovely and even lovelier

Than day blest with sunny daring masterful

I'm not yet sure of my preference personal

Is it caprice that tempts me towards starry night easeful

Or is it the good sense that persists continual?

A whisper is in the air: oblivion is blissful

In The Context Of Easter

After a flood of "Hosannas", you were crucified O Lord!

You, for a moment, pleaded with Father to take away the cup bitterest

In bitter pain, you wept aloud, "Why did Thou forsake me? "

O Jesus, you uttered the anguished syllables of the multitude

At the last moment, in happy surrender, you whispered fulfilment

The entire Humanity would love to believe in Resurrection magnificent

That belief is fed by heroic hope, set free from Satanic armada accurst

Let us rage against blasphemous currents, and sing "Hallelujah", love-lit

Surrender

The urge to excel is to be extolled with harp and lyre

Heaven gets created by the longing eternal for the ethereal

Life's eternal longing for itself constitutes Universes blissful

Even silence is alive with throbbing, soulful notes beautifully lyrical

In a dream daringly human, we see the dust blooming and ourselves immortal

O Lord, won't you forgive us, as we indulge in our fond follies for a little while?

At your mighty trumpet call, we leave our toys and surrender sobbing, tearful

Sequence

We wonder at sequence inexorable

And offer salutations to the ethereal

In happy surrender to the inevitable

Raging against the inevitable: is it advisable?

Would we accept the constitution of silence eternal?

We are the evidence of life's longing for itself primordial

Let us extol ourselves as waves in the ocean wonderful

Or as birds in the sky, though the sky entire eludes us tactful

Let us indulge in occasional vanities and lyrical notes fanciful

And at last merge serenely with the ocean or the skies awful

The Rich Sinner

The poor sinner gets transfigured into a rich one,

When he feels forgiven, and a fabulously rich one,

When he forgives himself, prompted by voices of redemption,

Breathed into the soul, earned deservedly by agonized contrition

Fed by the conviction: there is no crown without crucifixion

Probably, the world is beyond the reach of our comprehension

Mysteries abide, and though we shall fly up to Heavenly Eden

Sometimes the blazing Sun shall pitilessly strike us down

Is it not Thou, O Lord, who put in us the longing for Eden?

With hearts burning, we dare ask Thee "Why are we now angels fallen?

We don't aspire to be angels, we would be content to be truly human

That we might indulge in occasional follies and fancies mundane

And at Thy command, O Heavenly Father, were turn to melodies solemnly human

Raised To Life

May all my utterances be fire-tongued, love-lit

That burn out all unforgiving wretchedness, hell-wrought

Melodies fabulously rich put out all foul notes damned

Voices ethereal constitute a blaze that reduces the Devil to dust

Waves soothing surge up, tongues of fire dance about

Breathing benediction, syllables blest burst out

All temptations to utter words maligned get buried

I find myself forgiven, raised to life benign, enthroned

Devotee

I wake up every dawn and greet the rising sun

Wondrous, with wonder thundering within me solemn

Chirping birds rouse in me sleeping gods benign

With attendant angels urging me to utterances real human

Yet I feel overwhelmed, awed, subdued and withdrawn

Slight strains of pain break out from within recurrent

Suddenly it dawns upon me: it is human to be a celebrant

Celebrate yourself, O Man, sing madrigals magnificent

Discover something refreshingly new in the familiar, eternally set

Blasphemer

To the lover, his darling is the goddess par excellence

When a slight smile dawns upon her cheeks, it is the heavenliest blossom

And if at all it fades out, he is thrown into utter chaos

And he would rouse gods to bring in redeeming grace

An onlooker might wonder what holds them together so close

Yet might envy their spirited soaring up to the skies

Their love-lit, intoxicated moves stir up mighty ecstatic waves

The extravaganza of love highlights human richness, the blessedness

Brand it folly or vanity, then, you are a blasphemer, sinner fallen from grace

Human Inadequacy

Wiping out tears is a human gesture

Worthy of adulation and recommended as means sure,

Yes, as a rare ladder leading to heavens austere

And in broader terms a human act meriting Paradise

If tears blood-shot flood out profuse,

Wiping them out with readiness, though laudable

Still should disturb the really conscientious

As it betrays the essential human inadequacy

Weeping bursts out from the hearts melted in furnaces

Confession

The glitter of Crown sometimes glitters with a glow false

Kingdoms sometimes rise up on shattered bodies of the righteous

I wonder how saints can enjoy bliss, despite wailing agonized from pits bottomless

Brand me a sinner for these blasphemous, unwarranted wanderings

O Lord, compassionate, bounteous, forgive me, the poor sinner these raging vanities

Grant me serenity to accept the constitution of silence with folded hands

Though I feel a saint should choose hell, I confess, O Lord! My craving for Thy bliss

Vision Benign

Give me the vision to delight in self awesome

To set in order the flood of Light immense,

The mighty waves of Love in serene sequence

When my vision fails, O Lord! I fall into chaos darksome

Raging vanities conspire to throw me into pits blasphemous

O Bounty bounteous, grant me serenity to bless Thee, ocean of blessedness

Deliverance

Mighty waves of bliss ethereal

Surge up in a sea shoreless, very real

Where I would love eagerly to dwell

In total abandon, beyond all turmoil

Setting cadences of love in order, breathing blessedly

Melodies break out from the Self, continual,

Constituting symphony spirited, hallowed, eternal

This is deliverance, getting beyond the ephemeral

Where bonds are no longer bondage inescapable,

But inspiring, bliss of togetherness, desirable

Revelation

The splendour of Kingdoms dazzle

The Earth-bound humans atremble

The Heavenward gaze brings trouble

And if the gaze strikes them blind inexorable

Mighty gods would let out a laugh of derision demoniacal

Prove these nightmarish notions false, O Lord, merciful

Blast out blasphemous whisperings with Thy thunder proverbial

May Thy Spirit benevolent descend upon us in a rush ceremonial

That we, Thy poor darlings stand rapt, blessedly blissful

Fully awake, awe-struck, absorbed in an air reverential

Still Singing Of Love

Please don't look for perfection

In the context of bestowal of affection

Mother bestows her benediction

Upon her little darlings even unto self-extinction

Despite their follies: the eager readiness to forgive

Constitutes the essence of love: the mystery of all creation

The overwhelming passion begets and sustains

All life, mortality slips into immortality benign

To look for perfection in the loved one

Is a sin, perhaps unpardonable and definitely unholy, inhuman

Heaven is where love reigns supreme, serene

Where all sprouts blossom forth, all melodies melt into One.

Brevity Intense

We all meet on the sea-shore splendid, fabulous

Let us greet one another in total abandon marvellous

May the bliss of being sustain us, despite all possible perils

Meeting stirs in us waves of ecstatic ecstasy

And don't allow ourselves be perturbed by thoughts

Of parting inevitable, the evanescence of all this

Instead, play gleefully, full of zest as long as it lasts

If the play be brief, that should inspire intense spiritedness

That is how we can make the miracle happen, the miracle of miracles:

The brief candle excels as a star resplendent, in all blessedness'

Love Intoxicates

Nothing intoxicates like love impassioned

No wonder, immortals woo mortals damned,

Even courting damnation in the course hallowed

The illimitable, in passion unbound, shrank downward

And opted to take upon himself bonds of Creation manifold

The entire Universe sprang up out of love infinite

The Lord was lured into romance wild with humans

In readiness to share the human agony unrelieved

Intoxicated love glorious prompted self-extinction exalted

Releasing a flood of light, infinitely infinite

Human Identity

Stretching our arms towards the exalted skies

As our eyes gaze upon the distant stars

Is a gesture magnificent, proclaiming human identity

The urge to rise up, to venture upwards constitutes beauty,

Yes, the beauty of being and that of becoming blest

All the while acutely aware of our limits inherent

And braving agonies ahead, we dare the illimitable

Some voices surprise us, are they subtle whisperings,

Set to trap us into sorry pits, or are they heavenly admonitions

Designed to lift us up, and set us totally free from fears and furies?

The Year Departing

I bid adieu to the departing year

Reverently, with harp and lyre, with my being entire

And would greet the unfolding New Year

With my eyes glistening, with heart aflutter

For all this is in the scheme of the Lord, ethereal

I often wonder who put in me longings immortal

Who willed the Tree of Life should sprout and bloom

Even as leaves wither or flowers fade out seasonal

The departing year kept me warm, despite winter occasional

And I would be grateful, if the New Year keeps me lovable

Dreaming

The collapse of dreams spells disaster gruesome

It is a fall from heights awesome

To sorriest pits darksome, real perilous

But the fall shouldn't deter us from dreaming

We should dream big, real fabulous

Waking up from ashes like phoenix mythical

There is rejoicing genuine in the act of dreaming

And its' a human privilege to spread out wings

And make leaps gigantic, though the sky entire is not ours

A Christmas Song

Jesus,

You were born in a manger O, Lord

Were you more pleased with the Crowned Kings' offerings

Or with the hearty, modest adulations of the shepherds?

We would love to believe most longingly

You would cheer up with greater elan when we sing falteringly

Than when heavenly angels sing spirited rhapsodies pompously

Later, you drove out the adulterers from your Father's temple

The only occasion you flew into fury, the compassionate, the ever gentle

Inspire us with love-lit hope, set us free to live daringly

And resurrect us with power and glory, grant us life abundantly

Beauty Mysterious

That sunset can be hilarious as sunrise

Nights can be blissful as days

Highlights the essential beauty mysterious

Immanent in life in the Universe awesome

Likewise, silence can be lovely as eloquence

Signals mystery unfathomable, inspires wonder wondrous

So let us sing with all possible spirited sweetness

Be confident notes lyrical shall keep ringing in blessedness

The Blessed

The blessed are those who parade spiritedly

Even when the skies darken unduly

Confident of the forthcoming rosy glow radiant

Yes, who get overwhelmed, surrendering themselves devoutly

At the altar built by themselves, prompted by urges holy

This sort of surrender assumes a glory triumphant

Sweet whisperings, as though in miracle mightiest

Suddenly burst forth into trumpet loftiest

Hallowed silence incarnate as eloquence magnificent

Set Free

If all the waters of bitterness

Gather at the valley of egoism

Then to exalt the valley gruesome

To heights blissful calls for daring humanism

Getting drowned in the waters is to court darkness

Laxity or vanity might invite tragic consequence

Self-cleansing agonizing might offer light benign

That lifts us up, guiding our vision towards heavens

And we are no longer trapped in the valley perilous

We are set free, to soar up infinite reaches

We Too

It should not unduly perturb us

That we are not in limelight awesome

Not particularly privileged, nevertheless,

Our spirited self can seize some space

And believe the stars sparkle also for us

And sunny mornings bloom marvellous

Eerie evenings and moon-lit nights fold us in embrace

We also may awaken harp and lyre with ease

Though our strains lyrical may not soar up skies

And our dancing steps or gestures may miss angelic grace

We can pat ourselves with pride that we are not vainglorious

Worthy Of Resurrection

By way of consolation, counsellors sodden in compassion

Would offer confirmed words of wisdom solemn:

"There is no crown without crucifixion"

In the human context, crucifixion doesn't always guarantee crown

Nevertheless, death and resurrection are often events in life

In our agony, we often weep aloud like Jesus crucified:

"Father, my Heavenly Father, why hast Thou forsaken me? "

And we are blessed, if we dare declare confident:

"Everything has been fulfilled", with a smile radiant

Falling into the sorriest pit, never to rise again spells death

May be vanity to assume the dust would bloom

Yet the hope elevates Man to the status human sublime

And makes him worthy of resurrection glorious

Don't Tempt Me Please

O Heavenly Father,

Give me the strength to defy Thy decree:

The decree to sacrifice my son, flesh of my flesh

On the mountain holy, the altar eerie

Don't tempt me with offers grandiose

Powerful enough to trap even the austere, staunch:

The splendour of Paradise, perennially free of blemish

May the spirit of the Son of Man who spurned Kingdoms glorious

Descend upon me with a rush mighty and penetrate me through and through

And set me totally free from the sin grievous: self-seeking unpardonable

Let me not be guilty of desecrating the altar, elevated status human

Missing

One who misses a lilac forever

Perhaps misses the bloom entire

Grieving over missing is human to the core

And that is what makes meeting so special and dear

Setting out with zest marks benediction

Aware of hurdles, fire and brimstone

Subtle whisperings, insinuations, drawn out daggers hidden

The pilgrim proceeds undaunted, blissfully serene

And his destination greets him as a genuine hero solemn

He can afford to forget whatever he missed:

The halls decorated or grandiose shows magnificent

As this forgetting brings him the pure joy of fulfilment

Envy

The first fratricide in history proceeded from envy

Cain couldn't forgive his brother Abel

Who won Heavenly Father's special love

Earlier, even the Archangel fell from grace

Growing restless over intimations of Man's advent

Probably, Jesus' assurance of many mansions in his Father's house

Sprang up, allaying any human anxiety related to space

Darwin's Theory of the survival of the fittest

Constitutes the closest ally of the concept, The Chosen People

Our humanism urges us to rage against all these

A voice startles us saying:

"This is like raging against death, the unalterable fact"

Maybe, it is folly not to accept reality, however gruesome it be

A flash suddenly descends upon us: "Envy is not wholly of the devil"

Lighting A Lamp

Let me light this lamp

And count myself blessed

Let me have no vanity unwarranted

To imagine the light I kindle aright

Is the blessed of all lights hallowed

And would illuminate the entire world

Nor should it dishearten me

With thoughts of insufficiency or incompetence

Spirited pursuit of light makes the miracle happen:

My eyes open and get glimpses of the marvels around

A Voice thunders out from the skies exalted:

'Beware of blindness, O Man, dispel darkness'

The Paradox Of Love

Love passionate imposes a burdensome burden

Not easy to shake off, still lifts you up towards Heaven

Heavenly Father took upon Himself, in Creation,

A Herculean burden in overwhelming passion

Close-knit hearts exult in union

Hallowed be it, lit with love and compassion

All ties solemn compel a sort of surrender,

A surrender, if need be, even to the extent of extinction

The beauty of love resides in its Ego-projection

With its simultaneous, saintly, paradoxical Ego- rejection

Greetings

Let us wake up and greet the dawn

That would blossom forth into morning benign

All the while grateful to the night easeful, serene

The blessed find night and day equally blissful

Fight out blindness and be militant

Then dark won't be any longer dark

If we sharpen vision, light would be our own

If we open ears, sweet cadences would be our own

A Look At The World

What is now beyond vision

Might emerge prominent later

What is now in focus clear

Might vanish altogether forever

Kaleidoscopic display in a dazzle of colour

Might all slip into a vast look vacant

All forms coalesce in formlessness absolute

Conversely, formlessness diverge into forms infinite

All beings derive from the Being Ultimate

The entire phenomena spring forth from the One

Parting is inevitable in the context of meeting

All melodies slide into silence hallowed

Yet silence breaks into melodies infinite

A faded rose sings of a past full bloom radiant

Oblivion is bliss, after a feast of experience divergent

Delusion

Almost everyone, in varied ages, has lamented;

The rare species of noble people,

O Lord, is on the verge of extinction

This lament springs up from delusion

The deluded notion of self-righteousness solemn

Nurtured in puffed-up moments in vain

Blessed souls would find everyone blessed,

Fit to be saluted, worthy of everlasting heaven

Even the worst sinner, in rare moments, could be a saint

Even archangel might, in weak moments, fall into sorriest pit

Creative Sport

O Lord, may the spark of Light

Within me flash out brilliant

Blooming forth as melodies love-lit

That would enchant the entire lot blest

May I be permitted to join the chorus hallowed

To establish the Kingdom of Light

At the darkest dark is a miracle,

A human feat, fit to be saluted

That elevates Man, stirring up straight

Envy even in celestial beings celebrated

In the Scriptures Sacred, for their fighting spirit

Cancelling out Hell, is indeed a creative sport

Towards Fulfilment

Though I may never reach the peak loftiest,

There is a certain joy very real in setting out.

Though I may never hope to excel a lark heavenly,

Let me sing out a note of my own, however worldly.

Though the garden I fondly raise lacks Edenic grace,

That is a garden nevertheless, and I can rightly rejoice.

Though all children are lovable and command my love,

It is right to love my children most indulgently, uniquely.

I shall be content with just a flower, though I dream of bloom

Birthright

Evil holds its sway on the world

As soon as we surrender sheepishly

Our own crown which adorn us deservedly

The crown thunders out our power and glory

To the resplendent skies and beyond

Be ourselves, dignified beings capable of humanity

No serpent would dare enter our garden lovely

And spoil its loveliness and make it accursed

Instead, humans would tempt darklings into light

And convince themselves of blessedness, their birthright

Everlasting Life

Life everlasting is no guarantee of bliss

As the Scriptures would subtly suggest

It can be eternal perdition, unrelieved anguish or angst

O Sweet Jesus, Love Incarnate why should we be resurrected,

We the poor devils, as we are, the easily tempted?

Why do Thee set us free to be condemned, damned?

What glory is there in getting a malady-ridden body resurrected?

We plead with Thee O' Lord, most compassionate

Better, reduce us to dust and consign us to oblivion

If our beseeching is irrational, pardon our folly, O'Love Incarnate

Ward Off Doom

Probably the hardest blow unbearable

Is the sudden flash of thought rushing in inexorable

I have nothing worthwhile to leave behind

Nor anything solid to cheer me even vainly

The burden of this blow would bury me in grave graceless

Even the most celebrated singer may not have sung to his heart's content

But it is gross misfortune conceivable not to have sung at all

Definitely it is doom not to have attempted spreading wings at all

While the skies were sunny, rosy and resplendent

Bloom blossoms forth even as you marvel at the skies longingly ardent

Peculiarly Human

Getting born into the World

Is it by Design? Or is it an Accident?

Design or accident, some find themselves in misery untold

While others, of course, a microscopic minority

Ride upon those who have the misfortune to be ridden upon

Perhaps, to dream, and that too extravagantly

Would launch poor darlings, earthlings

On orbits peculiarly human, set within limits

Forgive us, O Powers that be, our daring fraught with agony

Grant us a moment's blooming ecstasy

And vanity heroic to imagine the dust blooming

Utterances

Fire-tongued utterances

Breed honeyed sweetness

Beyond already set imaginings

Inspiring wakefulness limitless

To leap heavenwards on wings

That would defy hell-fire sparks

Possibly gods would envy Earthlings

And in an impossibly benign moment

Would be gracious enough to forgive them

And would exclaim: ' you are no longer poor darlings

On the other hand, indeed rich, fabulously rich

You set us wonder, wondering thunderous'

The Damned Kiss

"Is it with a kiss that you betray me? "

The piercing agony of getting betrayed

Gets further sharpened by the mode:

By a kiss, a human gesture of love profound

If Judas had even hit Jesus or spat on the face

The pain would have been, perhaps less

O Sweet Jesus, Love Incarnate, Saviour

Why did Thou permit Thy hitherto trusted disciple

To throw himself into the furnace of fire and brimstone

Burnt alive, buried alive, in graceless grave

Unable to forgive himself, self-condemned, damned

Perhaps, we are all wrong in our judgment

At last Judas acknowledged the enormity of his guilt

The all-forgiving Lord would embrace him into his fold

Sailing Through

Grant me serenity

To pierce through clouds unyielding

Despite voices slipping into shrieks

All forbidding and darksome

Until I perceive skies gorgeous

And it dawns upon me in a moment bounteous

Those who rejoice in sunset and sunrise

Sailing through clouds appallingly awesome

Would reach the Promised Land and find themselves at ease

Tower Of Babel

O Lord!

When Thou made communication obscure

Among the enterprising multitude

Busy building the Tower of Babel

What message did Thou signal?

Multiplicity of tongues, their variety so beautiful

O, in fact, isn't human voice set at ease

More seductive in its varied tones resourceful

Than in a single tone or strain monotonous?

Did Thou actually mean to set limits

To our soaring upto the skies awesome

Or awaken us into more worthwhile pursuits?

Yes, it dawns upon us now, in a glance:

The Kingdom of Heaven is on loftier peaks truly awesome

Angels & Earthlings

Singing is daring out at its noblest

Lost in the sweetness seductive

One may lapse into oblivion

That spells bliss both for the singer and the listener

Of course, songs can be of all sorts

Rhythmic beats set in cadences right

Could bring all angels down to Earth

Whispering among themselves mildly indignant

Baffled at the variety of strains precisely Human

'O Lord, how these mortals excel us in resourcefulness

They sing of ecstasy and of agony and stirrings of variety infinite

Whereas we the celestials sing the same strain forever and ever

If this smacks of blasphemy, we beseech Thee, don't be hard on us

Celebrations

If your birth is blessed, you can celebrate your birthday

If your birth is cursed, you find yourself whimpering all along

For some, every enviable avenue is wide open,

While some find all options closed forever

Some find themselves born in wrong places

That too, at the wrong juncture of history

For no conceivable reason, some are denied even breathing space

While some others strut about, occupying the entire space

Some are victims of unrelieved suffering gruesome

While others enjoy undisturbed, full-throated ease

O Love Supreme, art Thou happy with Thy design awesome?

The New Year Musings

Let us look forward to Morning wondrous

That would greet us with benediction marvellous

May the Powers that be forgive our romance,

Dreaming of human feats worthy of heavenly bliss

The daring vanity to conceive of bloom in doom

On this dawn of the New Year, the dear departed move us into sobs

Subterranean stirrings unleash a flood of bitterness

Sheer agony of brethren, O Lord, breed in us distress

Touch us and heal us, bless our rejoicings, celebrations

The Sacred Heart

Our stirrings weave the web

Of our self, burying or resurrecting us as the case be

A kaleidoscope, dancing capricious

'Set these steps in order, O Powers that be'

Out of Thy bounty extravagant, grant us grace

Exceedingly great that we may rejoice

In our attuned stirrings that take us

Straight to the Sacred Heart of the Universe

Whisperings damned would set the Heart bleeding

Nevertheless the blood hallowed would wash us clean

The all-forgiving Love would embrace us

So let us sing a song of love, dancing around with bliss

Martyr

Who holds on to hope

Despite getting thrown into pain and peril unendurable

Who is sure of Morning radiant

Blossoming forth even in the darkest dark

Who confidently contemplates

How to sing about and dance around even in densest pitch-black

Who thunders out militantly

Against subterranean stirrings murderous

Is the true martyr,

The privileged inheritor of the Kingdom of Heaven

Seize The Key

Retire into solitude if you are uneasy with multitude

Voices crash in upon you like capricious waves irreverent

Noise drives you crazy, scared and you seek asylum in silence

And if silence frightens you, what is the way out?

Then even your mightiest saviour would concede defeat

You are yourself a master of whispers sweet and declarations thunderous

O man, true it is: sometimes silence can be treacherous

No angel would offer you the key to paradise

You should seize the key, daring fire and brimstone

Those ever willing to dare Hell shall find themselves

Quite at ease in Paradise, they opened themselves

The Tempter or The Tempted

The tempter and the tempted get united

In a frenzy of kinship most intimate

Deluded this evil delight lasts life-long or even beyond

In spring, blooms seduce even Puritans militant

Sweet scents and petals soft, extravagant

Passions run riot and move mountains

Chaos breaks out, dazzle of colours blurs out vision

Rhythm natural, serenely sweet slip into roars violent

Devotees would have us believe in Design immaculate

In this world where sinners and saints move about

O Lord, wasn't Thou that made the combat inevitable?

The baffled humans dare ask Thee:

Whom would Thou favour, the tempter or the tempted?

The Perfect End

When we awake harp and lyre,

We are keen to strike the notes sweetest

When we sing in our voice,

We wish to sing with full-throated ease

Our mortality slips into immortality,

As our notes settle in the skies

When we sing or strike the last note,

We embrace silence, get merged with the Universes

A blessed soul gets joyfully surprised:

Yes, even silences sing

Passion gets dissolved in an ocean of compassion

Waves subside, peace presides

Prof Varghese J Kuttikat is a retired Principal& Professor of English at Kodungallur Kunhikuttan Thampuran Memorial (KKTM) Government College in Kerala, India. He has published several acclaimed poetry books including:

- *'Enchanted Songs'*
- *'Let Me Sing'*
- *'Little Jean'*
- *'Revelations'*

www.ingramcontent.com/pod-product-compliance
Lightning Source LLC
Chambersburg PA
CBHW081559040426
42443CB00014B/3404